T0341293

"Dr Plum Hutton has used her wealth of knowledge and experience of dyslexia to deliver a book which is informative but also amusing and captivating for children. Weaved throughout the story are the challenges faced by the hero who has dyslexia, but his strengths are highlighted as he saves the day! The accompanying guidebook provides helpful questions to challenge thinking in this area and offers valuable information about this specific difficulty."

Jane Jackson,
Head of Learning Support,
Dragon School

"It has been so refreshing to read such a clear explanation of the different aspects that make up the dyslexia concept. This is a gift to parents and schools who need a professional but easy-to-digest understanding of dyslexia. This understanding is then put into a living context, by the hilarious, imaginative and emotionally intuitive story about a child surmounting the barriers that dyslexia-type difficulties can cause. The activities that sit alongside the story make this 'package' a wonderful and pragmatic resource for parents and schools."

Caro Strover,
Educational Psychologist

"I can honestly say I now know an awful lot more about dyslexia and the unique challenges it brings – it was a really interesting, accessible read and will be useful both personally and professionally. Thank you!"

Emma Judge,
Parent

"*A Nasty Dose of the Yawns* is beautifully written, illustrating how difficult it can be for a child or young person living with dyslexia. The story is heart-warming, empathic and yet filled with humour. It provides subtleties of how adults can support a young person struggling to read and write, focus on their strengths and maintain confidence and self-esteem. The book appeals to school pupils and adults alike.

The supporting guide, which is evidenced-based, provides very useful and pragmatic strategies and guidelines on how best to support pupils who have dyslexia. The story and the supporting guide perfectly complement each other."

Karin Twiss,
*Senior Educational Psychologist
and Strategic Lead for Autism and
Neurodevelopmental Conditions*

Supporting Dyslexia and Literacy Difficulties in Schools

This guidebook, designed to be used alongside the storybook *A Nasty Dose of the Yawns*, has been created to educate readers on the practical, social and psychological impacts of dyslexia on children and young people.

Providing an easy-to-read introduction to dyslexia and literacy difficulties, this resource is rooted in theory and takes a holistic approach to supporting children with dyslexia. Chapters cover not only strategies to support literacy before and during their school lives, but also offer an understanding of the emotional challenges that come with struggling to master a skill that other people pick up so easily.

Key features include:

- an accessible guide to dyslexia and literacy difficulties
- chapter-by-chapter discussion points for use with *A Nasty Dose of the Yawns*, supporting young people's reading of the story, helping them to understand dyslexia and encouraging them to recognise their strengths
- case studies and strategies to help parents and practitioners recognise the challenges faced by children with dyslexia, and to provide additional support.

This is an essential resource for parents, teachers and other professionals supporting children aged 8–12 with literacy difficulties or dyslexia.

Plum Hutton is a chartered educational psychologist and former learning support teacher. She holds a doctorate in educational psychology. She has more than 15 years of experience working as a local authority educational psychologist and latterly has transferred to independent practice. Through her work she has pursued and delivered training on many areas of professional interest, including supporting children with persistent anxiety, attachment difficulties, literacy difficulties and sensory processing differences.

Plum is a keen storyteller. She has gathered inspiration for her writing from her work, the challenges of parenthood and also through a nomadic existence as an Army wife, which has taken her to many locations across the UK and as far afield as East Africa.

Adventures with Diversity

An Adventure with Autism and Social Communication Difficulties: *The Man-Eating Sofa* Storybook and Guidebook

The Man-Eating Sofa: An Adventure with Autism and
Social Communication Difficulties

Supporting Autism and Social Communication Difficulties in Mainstream
Schools: A Guidebook for *The Man-Eating Sofa*

An Adventure with Dyslexia and Literacy Difficulties: *A Nasty Dose of the Yawns* Storybook and Guidebook

A Nasty Dose of the Yawns: An Adventure with Dyslexia and
Literacy Difficulties

Supporting Dyslexia and Literacy Difficulties in Schools: A Guidebook for
A Nasty Dose of the Yawns

An Adventure with Childhood Obesity: *Down Mount Kenya on a Tea Tray* Storybook and Guidebook

Down Mount Kenya on a Tea Tray: An Adventure with Childhood Obesity

Supporting Childhood Obesity in Schools: A Guidebook for
Down Mount Kenya on a Tea Tray

Supporting Dyslexia and Literacy Difficulties in Schools

A Guidebook for
A Nasty Dose of the Yawns

Plum Hutton

Illustrated by Freddie Hodge

Routledge
Taylor & Francis Group

LONDON AND NEW YORK

Cover image: Freddie Hodge

First published 2022
by Routledge
2 Park Square, Milton Park, Abingdon, Oxon OX14 4RN

and by Routledge
605 Third Avenue, New York, NY 10158

Routledge is an imprint of the Taylor & Francis Group, an informa business

© 2022 Plum Hutton and Freddie Hodge

The right of Plum Hutton to be identified as author and Freddie Hodge to be identified as illustrator of this work has been asserted in accordance with sections 77 and 78 of the Copyright, Designs and Patents Act 1988.

All rights reserved. No part of this book may be reprinted or reproduced or utilised in any form or by any electronic, mechanical, or other means, now known or hereafter invented, including photocopying and recording, or in any information storage or retrieval system, without permission in writing from the publishers.

Trademark notice: Product or corporate names may be trademarks or registered trademarks, and are used only for identification and explanation without intent to infringe.

British Library Cataloguing-in-Publication Data
A catalogue record for this book is available from the British Library

Library of Congress Cataloging-in-Publication Data
A catalog record has been requested for this book

ISBN: 978-1-032-07639-3 (pbk)
ISBN: 978-1-003-20807-5 (ebk)

DOI: 10.4324/9781003208075

Typeset in Avenir and VAG Rounded
by Deanta Global Publishing Services, Chennai, India

Contents

Acknowledgements ix

List of Abbreviations x

1. Introduction 1

A Note on the Language Used in this Guide 1

Synopsis of *A Nasty Dose of the Yawns* 2

The Main Messages in the Story 4

2. Understanding Literacy Difficulties 5

Some Causes of Literacy Difficulties 6

Specific Difficulties with Literacy/Dyslexia 7

3. The Psychological Impact of Dyslexia 11

Low Self-Esteem 13

Anxiety, Stress and Depression 14

Disruptive Behaviour 16

Cognition and Executive Function 17

Impact on Parents and Family Relationships 18

Poorer Life and Employment Outcomes 19

4. Using *A Nasty Dose of the Yawns* to Promote Discussion 20

Chapter One 20

Chapter Four 24

Chapter Five 25

Chapter Seven 26

Chapter Nine 29

Chapter Ten 30

Chapter Eleven 31

Chapter Twelve 32

5. Supporting Children with Early Literacy Skills   **34**

Supporting Children Before They Start Formal Education   34

Early Support When Children Start School   36

6. Supporting Children with Persistent Literacy Difficulties   **37**

General Strategies   37

Role Models with Dyslexia/Literacy Difficulties   39

Hearing and Auditory Issues   41

Visual Issues   43

Reading   45

Spelling and Writing   46

Phonic Skills   49

Working Memory   50

Speed of Processing   52

Executive Function   53

7. Conclusion   **56**

References   57

Acknowledgements

I would like to extend my thanks to:

Iona and Ramsay Hutton for their encouragement and youthful perspective

Claire Anson, Karin Twiss, Fran Townend and Emma Judge for their support and advice

Alex Hutton for his patience, optimism and support during the writing of this book.

List of Abbreviations

ADHD   attention deficit hyperactivity disorder

ASD   autism spectrum disorder

DCD   developmental coordination disorder

DLD   developmental language disorder

1. Introduction

This guide is intended to be used with the storybook *A Nasty Dose of the Yawns*, an escapade where the main character has significant difficulties with literacy. The story is fun and adventurous and is likely to appeal to children of approximately 8–12 years old. It also highlights some of the issues faced by learners who find literacy unusually difficult. This includes the practical challenges of struggling to read and write in a society that takes adult literacy for granted. In addition, the psychological impacts of struggling to achieve a skill that most children acquire with relative ease are explored.

A Note on the Language Used in this Guide

A Nasty Dose of the Yawns is set in Year 6 of a primary school. The content of this guidebook is therefore most suitable for individuals of approximately 11 years of age, and the term 'child' has been predominantly used throughout the guide rather than 'young person'. However, many of the strategies would also be relevant to pupils in the first few years of secondary school.

It is acknowledged that children with literacy difficulties may find it difficult to read *A Nasty Dose of the Yawns* independently as it contains a wide range of vocabulary to hold the interest of older readers. However, it could be accessed through paired reading, or adults could read the story to children who do not yet have the skills to read it themselves. To aid children who find reading laborious, the story is shorter than other tales in the Adventures with Diversity series.

The language used to discuss neurodiversity and literacy difficulties is continually evolving. Therefore, readers are advised to keep up to date with any changes in terminology.

DOI: 10.4324/9781003208075-1

Synopsis of *A Nasty Dose of the Yawns*

Zack is an 11-year-old boy who finds school challenging due to being dyslexic. As a younger pupil, he was renowned for his anger, which was a consequence of repeatedly failing at literacy tasks. However, his Year 3 teacher, Miss Hazel, recognises that his troublesome behaviour was a response to his difficulties with learning and she teaches him strategies to help him to make progress and to manage his frustrations. The story begins on a sunny morning during Creative Arts Week, with Miss Hazel (who now teaches Year 6) planning fun activities for the day. Unfortunately, Zack is at the hospital that morning having his hearing checked.

Miss Hazel is unaware that an ancient, hairy creature called an ofsted has been living in the back of her art cupboard. The ofsted is accidentally brought out into the class in a bundle of tissue paper. While attempting to escape back to the cupboard, he shakes his long fur and covers the class in a strange yellow powder. This infects the whole class with a serious sleeping sickness, from which he has been suffering for many years. He scuttles unseen back to his hiding place, while the class falls into a deep sleep. Meanwhile, Zack has had a long wait for his hearing appointment and then witnesses an unpleasant encounter between his mother and Traffic Officer Simms, who tows away her car, because she was unable to read the parking signs and so parked in the wrong place.

The headteacher is horrified to find the whole of Year 6 in a coma and is desperate to deal with the problem discreetly, to prevent panic among the parents and pupils. She calls on the unctuous Dr Bling from the health centre next to the school, and together they try to solve the mystery and make a plan to manage the situation.

Zack returns to school in a black mood and is surprised to find that his friends are unconscious and, for the moment, no adults are in sight. With some quick thinking, an encounter with a slug and a bit of luck, he establishes that the mystery illness is caused by the yellow dust that has settled over the class. He carefully hoovers this up and, in doing so, revives the class. As a result, it appears that the headteacher and Dr Bling were involved in a strange hoax when they call the emergency services. Zack secretly empties the yellow dust from the vacuum cleaner into a bag and takes it home.

He decides to take revenge on Traffic Officer Simms by giving him a box of chocolates (having injected a small quantity of the yellow dust into the centre of each chocolate). The plan has a much greater impact than Zack intended, as Traffic Officer Simms feels obliged to share the chocolates with his colleagues and all 19 traffic wardens are rendered unconscious for several weeks. The incident stimulates Zack to develop an interest in chemistry and he trains as a doctor as he matures. He experiments on the yellow dust and develops a radical new sleeping pill that is used to help people who are recovering from accidents and operations. When asked how he developed his medication, he explains that it was with the help of three slugs and a traffic warden, but the details of the story remain his secret forever.

The Main Messages in the Story

- Difficulties with literacy are common. They can cause significant frustration, low self-esteem and academic underperformance.

- Children may demonstrate challenging behaviour as a way of distracting from their difficulties or as a means of venting their frustration.

- Dyslexics often feel that others make judgements about their intelligence based on their literacy difficulties. Therefore, when their problems with literacy are highlighted in public, they may feel embarrassed and foolish.

- However, children with literacy difficulties may have a range of strengths in other areas. It is important to provide opportunities for them to show these strengths.

- Adults can really help by recognising the difficulties and providing support. Good levels of assistance often significantly reduce the negative emotional consequences of dyslexia.

- There are lots of ways to support children who find literacy difficult and most people learn strategies to overcome the majority of their issues.

- Modern technology provides many ways to help learners with literacy difficulties.

2. Understanding Literacy Difficulties

It is estimated that human speech developed approximately 150,000 to 200,000 years ago. The ability to speak is believed to be an inborn function of the brain, like walking and breathing (Milne, 2005). However, reading and writing are much more recent inventions. Writing is about 4,000 years old and the human brain has not had time to evolve so that it acquires these skills naturally (Milne, 2005). As recently as 1820, it is estimated that only approximately 53% of the British population over the age of 14 were able to read and write (Roser & Ortiz-Ospina, 2018). Reading is not a skill that just develops as we mature; it is an artificial process that takes the brain many years to properly acquire. There are many underlying cognitive skills that are required to successfully learn to read and write, and it usually takes about a decade of practice to ensure swift automatic word recognition. Therefore, it is not surprising that some people have difficulties learning to read.

Learning to read and write in English may be particularly challenging because many of the words are not spelt in the way that they are pronounced. The same sound may be spelt in many different ways – e.g. 'rain', 'reign' and 'rein'. Alternatively, the same letters may be pronounced in many different ways. For instance, consider the different ways that the letters 'ou' are pronounced in the following words: 'flour', 'through', 'though', 'thought', 'borough' and 'hiccough'. This makes English significantly more complicated than languages such as Spanish, Italian and German where the words are usually spelt as they sound. In these languages, learners may be more likely to show issues with reading fluency and grammar, whereas spelling is a more frequent problem in English.

DOI: 10.4324/9781003208075-2

Some Causes of Literacy Difficulties

Children may experience difficulties with literacy for a range of reasons including the following:

- problems with eyesight

- issues with hearing

- poor educational opportunities

- general difficulties with learning

- speech and language difficulties, limited vocabulary or poor pronunciation

- English as an additional language

- poor levels of literacy among parents/carers

- lack of access to books/written text at home

- specific difficulties with literacy/dyslexia.

Many children swiftly overcome early troubles with literacy. For instance, children who have limited access to books at home often make rapid progress when they start school. However, some children experience specific difficulties with literacy that prove to be persistent despite appropriate intervention. This is often described as dyslexia. This is the case with Zack, the main character in *A Nasty Dose of the Yawns*.

Estimates of the prevalence of dyslexia vary, but it has been proposed that approximately 10% of the population have mild dyslexia and about 4% have more severe difficulties with literacy (Crisfield, 1996). Hence, it is likely that all schools, and most classes, will have some children who have difficulties with literacy.

Specific Difficulties with Literacy/Dyslexia

Persistent specific difficulties with literacy, often called dyslexia, are perhaps the most well known and most prevalent of all educational difficulties. There is no doubt that some children find learning to read and write more difficult than would be expected given their intelligence and school experience (Elliott & Grigorenko, 2014). Many people think that dyslexic learners have a distinct pattern of difficulties. However, despite a huge amount of research, it has proved challenging to produce an exact definition of dyslexia that is based on scientific findings (Elliott & Grigorenko, 2014).

In 2009 the British government published an independent report called *Identifying and Teaching Children and Young People with Dyslexia and Literacy Difficulties* by Sir Jim Rose. This report was influential and included the following working definition of dyslexia, which is still often used in the UK:

- **Dyslexia is a learning difficulty that primarily affects the skills involved in accurate and fluent word reading and spelling.**
- Characteristic features of dyslexia are difficulties in phonological awareness, verbal memory and verbal processing speed.
- Dyslexia occurs across the range of intellectual abilities.
- It is best thought of as a continuum, not a distinct category, and there are no clear cut-off points.
- Co-occurring difficulties may be seen in aspects of language, motor co-ordination, mental calculation, concentration and personal organisation, but these are not, by themselves, markers of dyslexia.
- A good indication of the severity and persistence of dyslexic difficulties can be gained by examining how the individual responds or has responded to well-founded intervention.

(Rose, 2009, p.29)

This definition has been found to be useful. In particular, it highlights that literacy difficulties occur across a range of intellectual abilities. It also emphasises that, rather than being a clear-cut category, literacy difficulties occur on a continuum, from very mild to severe. Therefore, a small number of children experience severe problems that may cause persistent difficulties throughout life. Others have moderate difficulties and some have such mild difficulties that it may be hard to determine whether an identification of dyslexia is appropriate or not, especially as early difficulties often improve as children mature. The Rose Report definition also highlights the importance of investigating how children respond to literacy interventions over a period of time, as a means of examining the severity of their issues.

The Rose Report definition has been subject to criticism. It clearly states that characteristic features of dyslexia are 'difficulties in phonological awareness, verbal memory and verbal processing speed' (Rose, 2009 p.29). While this is the case for many children with literacy problems, others do not fit this pattern and yet still display persistent difficulties with literacy. In addition, a common perception among the general public is that dyslexics frequently experience visual difficulties, such as letter reversals and problems seeing text clearly. The Rose Report definition does not refer to any type of visual difficulty.

> I used to find reading incredibly difficult until, in Year 1, my eyes were tested, and it was found that I needed glasses. It is much easier to read if you can see clearly! I hadn't realised how fuzzy everything had become, because for me it was normal.
>
> Year 5 pupil

The British Dyslexia Association added an additional paragraph to the Rose Report definition which effectively widens the definition even further. It states:

> In addition to these characteristics:
>
> The British Dyslexia Association (BDA) acknowledges the visual and auditory processing difficulties that some individuals with dyslexia can experience and points out that dyslexic readers can show a combination of abilities and difficulties that affect the learning process. Some also have strengths in other areas, such as design, problem solving, creative skills, interactive skills and oral skills.
>
> (British Dyslexia Association, 2010)

It has been suggested by Elliott and Grigorenko (2014) that perhaps the reason dyslexia has been so difficult to define is that learning to read and write is a complex process. Individual children may have difficulties with literacy for a range of reasons. Therefore, rather than being a clearly defined medical diagnosis, it has been argued that dyslexia is a socially constructed concept that has developed to acknowledge the significant difficulties that some people experience with literacy. Elliott and Grigorenko (2014) suggest dyslexia is perhaps best thought of as an umbrella term that indicates that a child has long-term difficulties with literacy, while recognising that the precise nature of the issues may vary from case to case. What seems to be commonly agreed is that when a child is finding literacy difficult, it is helpful to provide additional support at an early stage. For many children, this help will be enough for them to overcome their problems. However, some children's difficulties are persistent, despite good-quality intervention, and it would be these learners who might be described as having a specific difficulty with literacy or dyslexia.

Persistent difficulties with literacy/dyslexia are often found in learners who also experience other difficulties such as:

- developmental language disorder (DLD)

- autism spectrum disorder (ASD)

- attention deficit hyperactivity disorder (ADHD)

- developmental coordination disorder (DCD).

All these diagnoses occur independently, but it is not uncommon for some children with these diagnoses to also have significant difficulties with literacy. It is perhaps unsurprising that learners who have a significant attention deficit may find it harder to focus and hence succeed with literacy tasks. Likewise, children who struggle with motor coordination and motor planning often find the process of handwriting very challenging. There is significant overlap between DLD and dyslexia as pupils with both these issues tend to have phonological difficulties. However, phonological issues are often less severe in children with DLD, and they typically have broader difficulties that affect their comprehension of language compared with dyslexic learners. It has been found that some children meet the criteria for both DLD and dyslexia (Snowling et al., 2019).

3. The Psychological Impact of Dyslexia

Persistent difficulties with literacy affect individual learners in different ways depending on the severity of their problems, how they respond to challenges in life and the way in which they are supported. It is well documented that dyslexia is often found alongside emotional and behavioural issues. As stated by Livingston, Siegel and Ribary, 'dyslexia has been associated with depression, anxiety, lower self-esteem, attention deficits and often, behavioural problems' (2018, p.107). Children experiencing persistent difficulties with literacy tend to view their issues negatively and this can be an obstacle to success unless they are able to reframe their feelings more positively.

> I went through primary school assuming that I was stupid. All my friends found reading much easier than I did, my writing was a mess, and I usually came bottom of the class in spelling. One day, we did a listening comprehension task where we had to listen to some information and then verbally answer questions about it. I had no problems with this and came top of the class, but the other children accused me of cheating because they assumed I wasn't clever enough to get a good mark. I hated the way that people made judgements about my intelligence because of my poor handwriting.
>
> An educational psychologist

One of the main skills that children are required to demonstrate at school is the ability to read and write. When completing a history essay, learners usually gather information by reading and then summarise their arguments in writing. In science, learners are required to write up experiments and need to be able to accurately

DOI: 10.4324/9781003208075-3

read different terms such as 'translucent' and 'transparent'. Literacy is even required in social situations to text friends, read a menu or when ordering something online.Because literacy is such a vital skill, both at school and beyond, young people with literacy difficulties frequently have their poor skills exposed in public, which may feel humiliating. There is also the issue that others make judgements about people's ability based on the quality of their written work, both in everyday life and via formal examinations. As a result, it is unsurprising that literacy difficulties and dyslexia are associated with a range of social, emotional and mental health issues including:

- low self-esteem

- anxiety, stress and depression

- disruptive behaviour

- problems with cognition and executive function

- poorer life and employment outcomes

- negative impact on parents and family relationships.

These areas are discussed in more detail below. However, it is encouraging that many of these issues can be minimised if literacy difficulties are recognised early and if children are well supported by their parents and teachers.

Low Self-Esteem

Poor self-esteem is one of the most common psychological problems that arise from dyslexia. Children with literacy difficulties may experience regular failure as they struggle to learn a skill that most of their peers seem to acquire with ease. They may work harder than their classmates and yet make slower progress, which in turn affects their motivation. The additional effort that must be employed by dyslexic pupils to complete the same task as their peers is often unnoticed. The common assumption that there is a link between literacy skills and intelligence may cause learners with reading difficulties to feel unintelligent. As a result, many people try to conceal their poor literacy skills, to protect their self-esteem, but they may encounter frequent problems such as being unable to complete forms, read road signs or write a coherent letter/email.

Dyslexic learners are more likely to attribute their success to external factors (e.g. luck or the teacher) rather than to their own skills or hard work (Humphrey & Mullins, 2002), often resulting in the feeling that they have no control over their future success. Dyslexics have been found to have lower academic self-esteem and higher levels of academic anxiety (Livingston et al., 2018).

These issues may cause emotional insecurity, self-doubt and reduced motivation. Therefore, it is important to provide opportunities for dyslexic learners to demonstrate their strengths. In addition, 'early identification and remediation increase both academic and emotional well-being of individuals with developmental dyslexia' (Livingston et al., 2018, p.119). However, some learners show little improvement despite good-quality interventions. In some cases, their progress is hampered by emotional issues, which make them reluctant to persevere with reading and to engage with additional support.

I started to build walls around myself. I suppose it was a form of protection. I did not see the point in trying so hard, as the failure kept coming. With it came lots of scrutiny and evaluation . . . I can remember this lady teaching me on a one-to-one basis. I just refused to let her in. The learning was intense one-to-one and in most cases should have helped. I suppose I saw it as a period of time to endure.

A company director and business owner

Anxiety, Stress and Depression

Many dyslexic learners experience significant emotional distress because of their difficulties. Internalising those feelings may lead to anxiety or stress, which may not be immediately evident to others. Depression is also associated with dyslexia (Lima, 2011). All these emotional issues may become more severe as children mature to adulthood because competent literacy skills are taken for granted in most high-income countries. Adult literacy rates in the UK are estimated to have been at 99% for the last 20 years (Macrotrends, 2020).

People who have difficulties with literacy often feel stigmatised and may have been stereotyped as being stupid, lazy or careless before their needs were identified. Negative early experiences can contribute to adverse views of school and, in some cases, school phobia and test anxiety (Livingston et al., 2018). In Western society, personal success is often measured by educational attainment, followed by success in a valued occupation. Both these measures tend to require strong literacy skills. Therefore, many people with literacy difficulties feel high levels of anxiety about their issues being revealed. Also attempts to hide problems with literacy may have the unintended consequence of learners not receiving the support that they need.

Children often report that the prospect of being asked to read aloud in public can cause them to feel considerable stress.

I can remember one occasion where I was asked to spell the word 'egg' in front of the whole class, and I just thought it was 'eg'. The teacher got cross with me in the end and yet again I had to leave the room. The class was laughing, and this is a difficult memory to recall. I suppose this was a low point for me . . . It was probably where I started to lose my confidence. Would I ever be able to be good at anything?

A company director and business owner

It has been found that concerns about how other people perceive literacy difficulties may cause greater emotional distress than the actual problems with reading and writing (McNulty, 2003).

Disruptive Behaviour

Dyslexia is associated with higher levels of disruptive behaviour than are usually found within the general population. Children may engage in poor behaviour due to the frustration that their difficulties create (Riddick, 2010). In addition, when learners find tasks very challenging, it is harder to sustain attention and motivation. Hence, there is a temptation to distract peers and engage in task-avoidance activities, such as endless pencil sharpening or organising resources, rather than completing the work.

Research shows that diagnoses associated with challenging behaviour are three times as common in children identified as having dyslexia compared with the general population (Livingston et al., 2018). There is also an increased incidence of attention deficit and hyperactivity disorder (ADHD) in dyslexic children. It is thought that these externalising behaviours are most likely due to the negative emotional experience of having persistent literacy difficulties.

Dyslexia has also been associated with social problems, poor self-regulation and experiences of bullying, discrimination and ridicule. These issues often increase throughout life and seem to be partly related to the attitudes of others towards people with cognitive difficulties. Unfortunately, poor conduct and issues with peers may affect the willingness of teachers and parents to support dyslexic children with their persistent literacy difficulties.

> Getting in trouble for disrupting lessons was a much easier option than trying to do the work and failing, yet again.
>
> Year 9 pupil

Cognition and Executive Function

Dyslexia is associated with cognitive deficits such as problems with verbal memory and poor speed of verbal processing. However, the emotional impact of struggling with persistent literacy difficulties can also affect learners' ability to use their thinking skills effectively. It is well known that anxiety can impair concentration and working memory skills (Moran 2016). Working memory is required to retain information for a short time while we use it. For instance, it is necessary to retain an instruction or hold a sum in one's head while carrying them out. If children are feeling persistently anxious, it becomes harder to use working memory skills, which may be a particular problem for dyslexic learners, who often have difficulties with verbal memory anyway.

Dyslexics are vulnerable to symptoms of depression and anxiety (Lima, 2011) and these are thought to negatively impact executive function (Snyder, 2013). Executive function is the term used for a group of mental skills that include working memory, flexible thinking and self-control. These skills are vital in order to function efficiently in daily life, as they allow us to plan and execute tasks, sustain concentration, follow directions and regulate our emotions. Therefore, emotional issues, such as anxiety, stress and low mood, will also make it harder for children to collect their thoughts and focus on schoolwork, which is something that dyslexic learners already find challenging.

> I still remember, while I was at university, the burning humiliation when the first letter that I wrote to a boyfriend was returned to me, with the spellings corrected in red pen.
>
> A teacher

Impact on Parents and Family Relationships

When a child is struggling with dyslexia, it can place pressure on family relationships. Parents often feel guilty that they may have passed on a genetic tendency to have literacy difficulties (Livingston et al., 2018). This may be compounded in cases where parents do not feel that they have good enough literacy skills to support their children.

When children have persistent difficulties with literacy, parents often want to help by providing specialist assessment and remediation. This can be expensive and put the family under financial strain. Family relationships can also be put under pressure before a child's difficulties have been identified, because parents may not understand the problem and therefore feel that the child is not concentrating or trying hard enough.

Parents and carers play an important role in protecting children from misunderstandings and the distress associated with literacy difficulties. Dyslexic children who perceive that their family is supportive show better self-esteem, life satisfaction, psychosocial adjustment and positive coping strategies. However, some parents may become so dedicated to supporting the child's academic progress that they may miss the need also to support their emotional needs (Livingston et al., 2018).

One study reported that dyslexic learners in higher education thought that the important adults in their lives considered them to be incompetent and unintelligent (Pollack, 2008). These perceptions persist, even though the young people must have achieved considerable academic success to have reached higher education.

Poorer Life and Employment Outcomes

Research has shown that people with poor literacy skills often experience poorer outcomes in life, such as higher levels of unemployment, poverty and offending behaviour (Bennett, 2008). High levels of dyslexia have been found among prison populations.

Individuals with dyslexia can underestimate their actual abilities and so may experience less success in life, due to their reduced expectations. Similarly, young people who start secondary education with very low literacy skills are five times more likely to be excluded and four times more likely to truant than their peers (Gross, 2008).

It is clear that persistent difficulties with literacy can have significant negative consequences. However, many of these can be minimised with early identification and support. Dyslexia is now a well-known difficulty, and it is much better recognised and remediated than was the case in previous generations. Nowadays, schools typically have experience of supporting children who find the acquisition of literacy challenging and will seek additional support in the few cases where children experience severe difficulties. Hence, with a combination of early identification, support from teachers and parents, and the use of technology (if required), it should be possible to greatly reduce the negative emotional impact of dyslexia. A range of ideas to support children with literacy difficulties is presented later in this guide.

4. Using *A Nasty Dose of the Yawns* to Promote Discussion

A Nasty Dose of the Yawns is an adventure story that is intended to appeal to all children. However, woven into the story is considerable information about what it is like to have dyslexia or persistent difficulties with literacy. Therefore, the book could be used to motivate those who are struggling with literacy by showing that learners can overcome problems and go on to succeed. In addition, the story is a useful resource to promote understanding and discussion among children, young people and adults who may not have considered the impacts of living with dyslexia. The following sections of the book are particularly relevant for readers who would like to encourage discussion about literacy difficulties. Some questions that could be used to promote debate are suggested below.

Chapter One

Miss Hazel recalls her first meeting with Zack. He was frustrated and angry because he had struggled with literacy for so long. Miss Hazel understands that his troublesome behaviour is a consequence of his persistent literacy difficulties.

How would you feel if you were asked repeatedly to attempt something that you found incredibly difficult? Why do you think that Miss Hazel had often seen Zack angrily pacing around outside?

- Having to complete tasks that are so difficult that a person rarely achieves success is often demoralising and leads to frustration and feelings of hopelessness. Zack experienced persistent failure in his early days at school, which made him angry and defiant.

DOI: 10.4324/9781003208075-4

What do you feel are your strengths?

- We all have different strengths. Try to encourage the children to think about a range of qualities – e.g. patience, determination, musical talent, good writing skills, sporting achievements, good social skills.

Do you think that we value some strengths more than others? If so, which ones and why?

- In the current education system, there is a tendency to formally recognise academic strengths over other qualities. This is partly because that is how the exam system measures success at school and because literacy skills are important in many workplaces.

Why might adults sometimes misunderstand children's behaviour? How does it feel when an adult asks your views and really listens to you?

- Misunderstandings can occur for many reasons. Sometimes children struggle to effectively explain the situation. At other times adults may jump to conclusions without realising that they don't know all the facts. Taking time to really listen to children can be very illuminating and rewarding.

Can you explain dyslexia?

- Given that professionals struggle to agree on a definition of dyslexia, this is a challenging question. The main point is that dyslexia is a *specific* difficulty with literacy. It may affect people in different ways – e.g. individuals may have problems with spelling, reading or writing as well as retaining and processing information. They are often able to overcome these issues with support and practice.

Why do you think that some parents feel guilty about their children having dyslexia?

- Dyslexia often runs in families, so parents may feel that they have passed on the difficulty to their children through their genes. Also, parents with poor literacy skills may feel guilty about finding it hard to support their children, or just sad that they are unable to solve the child's issues.

If people find reading and writing difficult, does it mean they are unintelligent? Can you explain your answer?

- No. Literacy difficulties are not necessarily connected to intelligence. It is possible to be highly intelligent and to find reading and writing challenging or to be good at reading and writing but to find complex problem-solving skills difficult.

How do you think your thoughts affect your feelings and behaviour?

- Our thoughts can have a big impact on our feelings and therefore our behaviour. For instance, two people walking home in the dark may react very differently when they hear an unexpected noise due to their thoughts. The first person may have watched a scary movie recently and think that the noise is something threatening. He would probably rapidly feel afraid and perhaps run home. The other person may be preoccupied about having lost her cat, so when she hears the noise, she may wonder if it is the cat and explore the noise with feelings of curiosity and hope.

How do you think you can help yourself to succeed by thinking positively?

- Positive thinking can be a powerful way to help us to feel calm and determined, and so help us to persevere and succeed. Thinking 'I can do this' is much more likely to be helpful than approaching a task thinking 'I can't do this, it is going to be a disaster'.

Why do you think it might be helpful to think of dyslexia as being a monster that is separate from a person, rather than being part of the person? For what other problems could you use this technique?

- When we are struggling with issues such as dyslexia, an illness, anxiety, low mood or anger, it can be helpful to think of the problem as being separate from yourself. That way, it is possible to acknowledge your feelings of frustration about the problem without feeling that you are the problem. It is a subtle distinction but can be powerful. For instance, when dealing with a child who is behaving in a challenging way, it is helpful to make clear that it is the behaviour that the adult dislikes rather than the child. Imagining the problem as a monster, storm cloud or prickly plant helps the child to visualise the problem and focus their negative feelings on the problem rather than on themselves. They can work with adults to try to tackle the problem together. For instance, 'The anger monster is causing trouble today. Let's go for a walk and plan how we are going to get him to settle down.'

Chapter Four

Zack is at the hospital having his ears checked. He also remembers visiting the optician.

What is glue ear?

- Glue ear is when the middle part of the ear canal becomes full of fluid. This makes it hard for the eardrum to vibrate and causes temporary hearing loss. It is quite common in children because their Eustachian tubes, which drain fluid from the ears down the back of the throat, are very small. Some children experience frequent bouts of glue ear, especially if they have a cold and are congested. In most cases, glue ear improves as the child matures.

Have any of you had ear infections or blocked-up ears? What did it feel like?

- It often feels as though noise is muffled, and some children may experience an uncomfortable pressure inside their ears. If the fluid in the ear becomes infected, it may cause considerable discomfort as the pressure inside the ear builds up, in some cases causing the eardrum to perforate (pop), allowing the fluid to be released out through the ear.

How might it affect a person's education if their hearing is muffled?

- Infants who experience persistent bouts of glue ear may have speech and language delay due to frequently not being able to hear clearly. It can also cause problems with phonological awareness because it is hard for the child to hear the different sounds. This in turn will make it harder to learn phonics. Children may also appear to have attention problems because they develop the habit of not listening to the teacher due to not being able to hear clearly enough to understand.

What do you think it would be like learning to read if the words looked fuzzy?

• It would be really challenging because many of the letters look similar, so it would be hard to tell them apart, particularly for a child who is learning to read for the first time (compared with an adult whose sight might become less clear once they are already a competent reader). Many children find the visual experience of reading difficult; they may find that black text on white paper is dazzling, that the letters appear to move around or that everything is blurry because they need glasses.

Chapter Five

The audiologist explains how Zack's Eustachian tubes work. Zack and his mother encounter a traffic warden who tows away their car because they were unable to read a sign.

What are the problems if the inner ear fills up with fluid?

• It tends to cause reduced hearing and may result in infection.

How do you think Mrs Snodgrass feels after meeting the traffic warden?

• Humiliated, upset, worried and frustrated. She is probably annoyed with herself for having made the mistake of parking in the wrong place and that she will now be late for work and must pay a fine as a result. She is probably upset by the way the traffic warden dealt with the situation and physically shaken up by falling over and bruising herself on the lamppost.

Why do you think she did not explain that she was unable to read the sign?

- She was probably embarrassed to admit that she had difficulties with reading, particularly as the traffic warden was unlikely to listen or be sympathetic.

What problems do you think adults might have if they are unable to read effectively?

- Poor literacy in adulthood can cause significant problems such as being unable to read signs, menus, websites, instructions for how to cook food, information leaflets and official information (e.g. bills and tax information) that may arrive by post or email. It also makes it difficult to gain formal qualifications and reduces employment options. It is assumed in our society that adults will be able to communicate in writing. Not being able to do so effectively is likely to lead to continual frustration and embarrassment.

Chapter Seven

Zack remembers feeling humiliated when Miss Crimpet, who was unaware of his difficulties, asked him to read aloud in assembly. He also thinks about how he has been supported by his family and friends. He is keen to be able to help others, instead of always being the one who needs support. He uses his good problem-solving skills (and a bit of luck) to solve a problem that had confounded a headteacher, a medical doctor and an educational psychologist.

How would you feel if you were asked to do something in public that you knew you could not do?

- Most people would feel anxious that they might make a fool of themselves and perhaps feel angry and humiliated.

What assumptions do you think people might make about a teenager who has poor spelling or messy writing?

- People might assume that the person was not intellectually able, perhaps had not had educational opportunities or had not worked hard at their literacy skills. They might think that the person had a specific difficulty with literacy/dyslexia.

How could you help a friend who finds reading and writing difficult?

- Being understanding and not teasing them about their problems.

- Being sensitive about their issues, so that they do not feel embarrassed in public.

- Doing paired reading with them, or perhaps reading out information that the person cannot access themselves.

In what ways are parents important in supporting children with literacy difficulties?

- Parents can help significantly by doing additional literacy activities at home. Reading with the child every day and doing a few minutes' additional writing practice can make a big difference.

- Reading *to* children helps to develop their vocabulary and therefore makes reading easier.

- Parents can encourage phonological awareness by drawing attention to the different sounds within words.

- Parents can encourage the use of supportive technology – e.g. audiobooks, electronic spelling games and developing typing skills.

- Parents can be a huge emotional support to help the child to maintain self-esteem.

How do you think Zack feels about his mother finding reading difficult?

- He is aware of her difficulty and feels sorry for her and is protective of her when she has problems.

- He may also, at times, be frustrated that he has perhaps inherited his difficulties from her and that there are times when she is unable to help him and cannot complete some tasks as easily as other parents.

Why is it important for people to have opportunities to give help as well as to receive it?

- For people to feel equal within a relationship, it is usual for each party to contribute. For instance, a person may work for someone in exchange for payment, or if you help someone, it would be usual for the person to help you in return at some point. For children who need additional support, it helps their self-esteem if they feel they are able to make a worthwhile contribution in return for the support they receive, perhaps utilising their strengths in art, sport, music, practical activities or social skills.

How do you think Zack felt about helping Miss Hazel and his peers?

- He probably enjoyed the challenge of solving the problem and being able to help the people who often helped him. It probably also made him feel good afterwards when he realised that he had solved a problem that had dumbfounded the adults.

Why do you think he didn't tell everyone about it?

- It is interesting that he did not take the credit for solving the problem. This may be because he is modest and not a show-off. He may have enjoyed having a secret and confusing Miss Crimpet and Dr Bling. He also realised that it would be best if his plans to use the yellow powder remained a secret.

Chapter Nine

Zack again demonstrates good problem-solving skills and yet he has difficulties writing a simple note. He perseveres using his father's computer and the positive self-talk that Miss Hazel has taught him.

In what ways can a computer help someone who finds writing and spelling difficult?

- Typing helps when pupils' writing is hard to read; the spell-check facility is also useful.

- Speech-to-text and text-to-speech software can help young people to communicate in writing and to read.

- There are many computer programs to help with literacy – e.g. Clicker, which supports reading and writing with the use of predictive text.

Did Zack make a good decision when he decided to inject the yellow paste into the chocolates? Explain your answer.

- It was a risky decision because he did not know what was in the yellow dust, what the long-term effects might be and what dose would be appropriate to send someone to sleep for a few hours. He also had not considered what would happen if one person ate lots of the chocolates.

Why do you think that Zack was a thunderous ball of anger when he was younger?

- He was so frustrated by his literacy difficulties that he had become persistently angry.

What does it mean when the text says 'Nowadays, it was hard to know if the mother was helping the son or vice versa'?

- Zack's literacy is improving and through the process of supporting Zack, Mrs Snodgrass's literacy skills are also getting better, so they are both learning together.

Chapter Ten

Traffic Officer Simms ridicules Zack's note because he has used the word 'except' rather than 'accept'. These words sound very similar but are spelt differently and have different meanings. Unfortunately, a computer spell-checker may not pick up this type of error.

Do you feel it is important to be able to spell correctly? Why?

- People do expect adults to be able to spell correctly, and it is considered a priority in formal examinations. It also makes work look unprofessional when there are spelling errors. However, much of English spelling is not very logical, and as young people are increasingly communicating using abbreviations via text, the accepted way of spelling words may change in the future.

How did Traffic Officer Simms react to the mistakes in Zack's note?

- He made fun of the errors and also made the incorrect assumption that the writer was not intelligent because of the spelling mistakes.

How might Zack have felt if he knew what Traffic Officer Simms thought about his note?

- He might have been embarrassed. However, Zack dislikes Traffic Officer Simms so much that he might not be too bothered about his opinion.

Do you think Traffic Officer Simms understands what it is like to have literacy difficulties?

- No, I suspect that he has always found literacy easy and therefore is dismissive of those who find it challenging.

Chapter Eleven

In this chapter Zack's chocolates cause 19 traffic wardens to fall into a coma.

Do you think it was a good idea to have done what Zack did? Why?

- No, it was potentially dangerous, and he could get in serious trouble with the police for deliberately intending to drug someone.

What other consequences could have occurred as a result of Zack putting the paste in the chocolates?

- Traffic Officer Sims might have eaten all the chocolates and died. He might have passed them on to another person. He might not like chocolate and throw them away.

What could Zack have done differently, to vent his anger with the traffic warden, but in a more acceptable way?

- It would have been better to write a letter of complaint to the traffic warden's superior.

Chapter Twelve

With the support of family and friends, Zack goes on to be a successful doctor. He is able to use his considerable intellect to overcome his problems and is a successful adult.

What do you think were Zack's strengths?

- He was quick to learn, good at problem solving, interested in the world around him, talented at maths and science, sociable and friendly.

In what way do you think Miss Hazel changed Zack's life outcomes?

- Zack had fallen into the pattern of feeling angry, frustrated and that he was a failure. He was gaining a reputation for challenging behaviour at school. When these issues are not addressed, it may lead to serious disaffection both with regard to education and later possible issues with breaking the law and difficulties gaining employment. Miss Hazel supported Zack to make progress and set his life on a more positive path.

Do you think it would be difficult to train to be a doctor if you have dyslexia? What might be the problems?

- It would be demanding because the training is academically challenging and the university courses are very competitive. Doctors are required to learn and retain large amounts of information; this could be difficult for someone with short-term memory difficulties – a common problem among dyslexics. It is also important that doctors can read and write accurately, so that they do not make errors when recording diagnoses or prescribing medication.

In what way do you think the support for children with dyslexia has changed over the last 100 years?

- It has been acknowledged that many people have a specific difficulty with literacy, despite appropriate teaching and good levels of intelligence. In the past, many children with literacy difficulties were assumed to be lazy or unintelligent. Therefore, their outcomes in life were often poor.

- It is understood now that early support from both parents and schools often helps children to overcome difficulties with literacy acquisition.

- Exam concessions such as additional time and a reader or scribe can be requested if appropriate, to allow pupils to demonstrate their knowledge despite having poor literacy skills.

- The negative emotional impacts of having literacy difficulties have been greatly reduced now that children's needs are usually acknowledged and supported.

5. Supporting Children with Early Literacy Skills

There are many ways to support children's early literacy skills. The following section includes a selection of ideas that could be considered when helping young children to learn to read and write.

Supporting Children Before They Start Formal Education

- There is evidence that children with good speech and language skills are less likely to have difficulties with literacy. Parents can help children from the first few weeks of life by supporting the development of speech and language – e.g. by regularly giving eye contact, talking, interacting, sharing picture books and pointing out items of interest. Adults can join in with children's play, perhaps narrating what the child is doing, to help them to put words to their actions – e.g. 'Look the train is going under the tunnel. Oh no! It's going to crash!'

- Reading to children from an early age shows them the purpose of books and can encourage a love of stories and information books. It also helps to develop joint attention skills, which aids young children in learning to attend to adult-directed tasks.

- Reading to children is also a good way to develop their vocabulary. Having a strong vocabulary is helpful when children are learning to read, because when they encounter an unfamiliar word, they are often able to partially decode the word and then guess, using the meaning of the sentence and their knowledge of vocabulary. If the word is not known to them, it is unlikely that they will guess correctly.

DOI: 10.4324/9781003208075-5

- It is helpful to develop children's listening skills and phonological awareness. This is the ability to hear the different sounds within words. For instance, the word 'cat' is made up of three sounds 'c-a-t'. It is helpful to draw children's attention to the different sounds that they hear in words – e.g. 'Bat begins with a "b". What other words start with that sound?' or 'What sound can you hear at the end of "bed"?'

- Engaging in music, songs and nursery rhymes is also a helpful precursor to reading because rhythm is an important element of all these activities.

- Rhyming words could also be explored as well as clapping the syllables in words and playing games such as 'I spy with my little eye something beginning with . . .' (pick a letter sound).

- It is easier for children to learn to hear the sounds within speech if they are not distracted by background noise. Try to avoid having the television/radio/music on in the background when talking with young children.

- Pre-school children can be encouraged to start to recognise some letter sounds, perhaps the letters in their name or of words that they frequently see written around them.

- Observe whether the child favours left- or right-hand dominance. For instance, if a pencil is placed on a table centrally in front of the child, with which hand does he/she usually choose to pick it up. Observe which hand the child prefers to use for craft activities, ball games, scissors, etc. If children favour using their left hand, it is helpful to provide scissors and pencil grips (if required) that are suitable for left-handed learners. Note: It is not uncommon for children to be undecided about their hand preference during their first year at school.

Early Support When Children Start School

- It is helpful if someone can listen to young children reading most days. This might be with a parent, grandparent, older sibling, family friend or school staff. It appears that children who read with an adult most days usually make better progress in reading than those children who do not often read at home.

- It may help if parents are made aware of how phonic skills are being taught at school so that they can reinforce these skills when reading with their child at home. Some phonic schemes encourage the use of a physical action to remind children of the letter sound, or the shape made by the letter when it is drawn. For instance, they might wave their hand in an 'S' shape like a snake and say 'SSSSS' when they encounter the letter 'S'.

- When supporting children with learning letter sounds, it helps if the adults are aware of the difference between the letter sound and the letter name. For instance, 'C' for 'cat' is the letter sound, but the letter name for 'C' is pronounced 'see'. Pronouncing letter sounds accurately is also helpful, without adding 'err' on to the end of the sound – for instance, when demonstrating 'c' for 'cat', try to avoid saying 'cerr' for 'cat'. Likewise, adults should be aware that vowels have short and long sounds. Hence, 'a' in 'apple' is the short sound and 'a' in 'ape' is the long sound, which is also known as the letter name.

- Because so many words in the English language are not phonologically regular, it is also good to help children learn to read and spell the 100 most high-frequency words.

6. Supporting Children with Persistent Literacy Difficulties

General Strategies

- It is usually helpful to speak with children (and their parents) who are finding literacy unusually difficult, to acknowledge the issue and plan how you will work together to support them.

- When trying to help learners with literacy difficulties, it is important to get to know them. This could include educational assessment and investigation of their cognitive strengths and difficulties. However, it is equally important to discuss with children their experiences of learning, what they feel they find easy/difficult, how they are feeling emotionally and whether there are any other issues (perhaps at home) that may be affecting their ability to learn effectively.

- When children are struggling with literacy, they usually spend many hours each week working on activities that they find really difficult. This can lead to a feeling that there is an emphasis on their weaknesses. Hence, it is important to seek out and celebrate their strengths in areas such as maths, problem solving, creative activities, sport, music, social skills, gardening, drama, dance and science. Acknowledging and valuing strengths is important to maintain children's self-esteem.

- It is often helpful to explain that some learners have a specific difficulty with literacy and to emphasise that specific difficulties, such as dyslexia, are not an indication of the person's intelligence. The aim is to give learners the confidence to discuss their difficulties and to seek help when required, rather than hiding their problems for fear of appearing to be foolish.

DOI: 10.4324/9781003208075-6

- Strengths can also be used to support specific deficits that a pupil may have. For instance, some children may have weak verbal memory skills but much stronger visual memory skills. Recognising strengths allows learners to use them to support the areas that they find more challenging.

- Children with literacy difficulties can feel a lack of self-worth if they frequently receive help and are unable to redress the balance by helping others. Therefore, it can be good to give dyslexic learners roles and responsibilities that allow them to use their strengths/ expertise to be useful or support others.

- Positive self-talk can be a powerful way to promote success. It is easy to start feeling negative when one finds something difficult. Unfortunately, negative thoughts, such as 'I can't do this', often impede our ability to succeed, by lessening our determination to persevere. It is helpful to aid children to become aware of their thoughts and the way in which positive thinking can help us to succeed. For instance, 'I can do this!' or 'If I do it step by step, I will succeed' or 'The teacher will help me if I get stuck'.

- It can be helpful to externalise learners' literacy difficulties, by talking as if they were a definite being/object. For instance:
    - *'Can you describe The Dyslexia?'*
    - *'If you imagined it as a thing or a monster, what do you think it would look like?'*
    - *'How does The Dyslexia affect you?'*
    - *'Let's work together to conquer The Dyslexia.'*
    - *'Gosh, The Dyslexia is causing trouble with this piece of work.'*

Talking in this way helps learners to think of the difficulties as being separate from their sense of self, rather than the child feeling that he/ she is the problem. It may also allow children to channel their anger and frustrations at 'The Dyslexia' rather than feeling angry with themselves.

- When pupils have significant difficulties with literacy that impair their ability to access examinations, it may be appropriate to apply for exam concessions. The rules surrounding exam concessions are reviewed every year, but it may be possible to request concessions such as extra time, a reader/computer reader, use of a laptop/scribe/ speech recognition technology, a prompter or supervised rest breaks.

- There is a wealth of technology available to help people with literacy difficulties. Assistive technology is rapidly developing, so it would not be appropriate to recommend specific devices or programs in this guide, but a quick internet search highlights the range of technology available. Organisations such as the British Dyslexia Association often review new technologies. Some poor readers find audiobooks helpful, and many pupils with handwriting difficulties find that use of a laptop or tablet greatly aids their ability to record their ideas. Many teenagers use smartphones to good effect for taking screenshots of written information, audio-recording instructions, dictating their ideas and setting reminders, etc.

Role Models with Dyslexia/Literacy Difficulties

It can be helpful to discuss role models of famous people who have succeeded, despite reporting to be dyslexic. Many historical figures described frustrations about not having their difficulties recognised and negative assumptions being made about their intelligence. Thankfully, dyslexia is much better understood and remediated these days.

There are many examples of successful people who struggled with literacy. Below are listed some adults who have openly spoken about their dyslexia and how they overcame their early difficulties:

- **Sir Richard Branson**: entrepreneur, author and founder of the Virgin Group which controls more than 400 companies.

- **Steven Spielberg:** film director, producer and screenwriter.

- **Jamie Oliver**: celebrity chef.

- **Keira Knightly**: actress.

- **Orlando Bloom:** actor.

- **HRH Princess Beatrice:** member of the British Royal Family.

The organisation **Made By Dyslexia** (madebydyslexia.org) has recorded interviews with many of the individuals mentioned above, where they talk about their issues and how they have found their dyslexia to be beneficial, as it has allowed them to think in a different way to neurotypical people. Many of these interviews are available on YouTube. It should be noted that the understanding and support for children with literacy difficulties has significantly improved in recent decades. Therefore, it is hoped that children today would not experience the same level of frustration with the education system as was the case for some pupils in the past.

Hearing and Auditory Issues

Some children have difficulties with literacy because they are unable to hear clearly. This may be because of a permanent hearing loss. Alternatively, many children suffer from intermittent reduced hearing due to glue ear. This is when the middle ear becomes filled with fluid, which makes the noise sound more muffled than usual and can lead to infection. Children who are frequently congested or prone to ear infections may have difficulties with glue ear. These issues often resolve as they mature and their Eustachian tubes become slightly larger and better able to drain fluid into the back of the throat. However, if their hearing has been poor at the time when they were developing language, it may affect their ability to hear clearly the different sounds in words – i.e. their phonological awareness. If children are finding literacy difficult, it is relevant to consider whether they are having any difficulties with hearing and, if necessary, to have their hearing tested.

It is helpful for caregivers and teachers to take note of behaviours that may indicate poor hearing such as the following:

• Frequently not responding when called, because the child appears not to have heard, rather than choosing not to respond or being absorbed in another activity.

• Being oblivious to quiet sounds.

• Often asking you to repeat what you have said.

• Choosing to have the television volume turned up high.

Any concerns about children's hearing can be followed up through their General Practitioner.

Another issue that may affect children is difficulties with auditory processing. This is when the child is able to hear adequately but has difficulties processing what they hear. A common problem is finding it hard to focus on what the teacher is saying, particularly against background noise. This can be a significant issue in schools, which are often noisy places with so many children in one building. When this is thought to be a significant problem, a test of auditory processing may be appropriate, rather than just a typical hearing test.

In school it may be helpful to do the following:

• Speak clearly and steadily.

• Encourage adults to face the children so that they can see the speaker's face and benefit from visual prompts such as facial expressions and lip-reading.

• Be aware of the impact of background noises such as the whirring of electrical equipment.

Visual Issues

Children should have their eyesight checked regularly because they may not realise if they are unable to see properly. Most children in the UK are offered visual screening at 4–5 years old at school. If this is not offered, it would be prudent to request an eye test by an optician and to continue with regular checks throughout childhood. Opticians will be able to check for a range of medical issues that may affect the eyes. When educational professionals work with children with literacy difficulties, they may encounter several issues that might affect a child's ability to read text efficiently and comfortably. For instance:

- Long- and short-sightedness. This may affect the learner's ability to see either objects that are close up, such as text in a book, or objects in the distance, such as what is written on the board.

- Problems smoothly tracking with both eyes along a line of text often causes children to miss out words or to skip lines. Following the text with a finger or using a reading ruler may help children to keep their place.

- Some learners say that they see double, particularly when looking at text that is quite close to their faces. In some cases, they may be experiencing convergence insufficiency. This is when the eyes struggle to come together to focus on an object that is brought close to the face.

- Some learners experience what is termed as visual stress, when they find black text on a white background glaring. Others comment that words appear to move around when they are trying to read.

If a child appears to have any visual difficulties with reading, their eyes should be checked by an eye specialist.

In school, the following strategies may be helpful to make the pupil's visual experience of reading as comfortable as possible:

- Books with a large font may help. This becomes more challenging as learners mature and start to read chapter books, where the text is generally smaller. However, it is typically possible to enlarge the text if reading an electronic book. Alternatively, it may be possible to use a page magnifier that magnifies the whole page.

- Some children find reading black text on a white background glaring. Printing information on buff-coloured paper, rather than bright white, may help with this. It is also possible to buy coloured acetate overlays that can be placed over the text. Some learners report that certain colours of acetates make the text look clearer. There seems to be limited research evidence that the use of coloured overlays makes a significant positive impact on reading progress. However, overlays are not expensive, and if individual children perceive that they are helpful, they may help them to feel more confident. If using an overlay, it is important to replace it if it becomes scratched and difficult to see through.

- If using an electronic book, it is often possible to alter the contrast settings, so that the writing is viewed on a grey background and is therefore less glaring.

Reading

It may be helpful to do some of the following:

- Read daily (if possible) with an adult. Paired reading (Topping, 1987) may be most effective, where the child and the adult take turns to read passages in a book. If the text is fairly easy, the learner can read the majority with the adult only doing an occasional word or paragraph. Adults can read a larger percentage of more challenging books.

- Read a mix of phonic readers and 'real' books, because children who make slow progress may become bored of books that are designed to mainly include phonologically regular words.

- Encourage the child to read the first 100 most high-frequency words automatically. These words are so common that they include approximately 50% of the words found in a typical children's book (Solity & Vousden, 2009). The words could be put on flash cards so that they can be frequently rehearsed.

- Break long words down into syllables so that they are easier to sound out.

- Continue to develop the pupil's vocabulary by reading *to* children, through conversation, discussion, explaining new words or asking learners to define or provide synonyms for interesting words. Avid readers encounter many more words than learners who find reading challenging.

- Encourage the use of audiobooks as they can allow poor readers to access books that are beyond their reading skills but may be popular among their peers or particularly appeal to their interests.

- Explore 'high interest – low reading age' books that are designed for children whose reading age may be below their chronological age.

Spelling and Writing

It may be helpful to do some of the following:

- Regular handwriting practice, preferably supervised by an adult, who can check that the pupil is holding the pencil in an appropriate grip and that the individual letters are being formed correctly.

- For most children, a tripod grasp is ideal, where the pencil is gripped between the index finger and thumb with the third finger supporting the pencil from below. Many children adapt this grip so that their thumb curls around their fingers. This makes it much harder to move the fingers when writing. For children who are struggling to settle on a good pencil grip, a wide range of rubber grips are available that can be slotted over the end of the pencil and encourage learners to place their fingers in the correct place.

- For children who have found it hard to adopt a reasonable pencil grip, an alternative grip may be helpful, where the pencil is placed between the index and third finger and then supported by the thumb. Although this may feel strange to begin with, it is surprisingly stable.

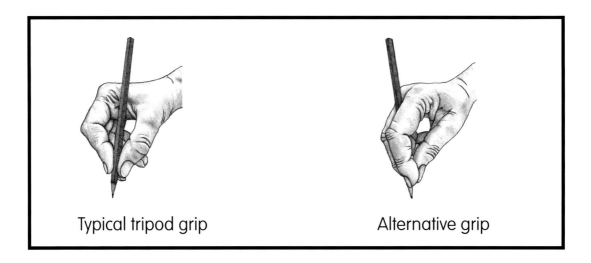

Typical tripod grip   Alternative grip

- When a pupil writes letters that are uneven sizes, it can be helpful to use handwriting paper (printed with four lines to guide letter sizes) or to mark the lines of normal lined paper with a highlighter pen to provide a visual guide of the expected height of the body of all the letters. Alternatively, children can practise writing using graph paper with small squares. They should place one letter in each square, which helps to keep the letters correctly sized and spaced.

- Teaching staff need to consider whether the aim of a particular exercise is for the learner to present coherently some interesting information or to demonstrate effective handwriting skills. If the emphasis is on producing a creative account, some children may benefit from alternative methods of recording for part or all of the exercise – such as through typing, use of a scribe, dictation, bullet points or annotated pictures.

- When marking work, it can help to focus on the positive aspects of the writing. If numerous spelling mistakes have been made, it may be best to only comment on a few of the more common errors that could be learnt or corrected.

- Children should be praised for using interesting vocabulary in their writing, even if the words are not correctly spelt.

- Some learners find typing easier than handwriting. There are many touch-typing programs available. It is helpful if children are supervised when first learning, to ensure that they are using the correct finger for each key. Typing is best learnt by practising little and often, ideally for a few minutes each day. When children can type faster than they can write, a laptop may be an effective alternative to handwriting for some work.

Learning to spell is arduous for some children. Multisensory techniques can be useful, partly because they often make spelling more enjoyable. For instance:

- Mnemonics: 'said' – **S**even **A**nts **I**n **D**anger, or 'because' – **B**ig **E**lephants **C**an **A**lways **U**nderstand **S**mall **E**lephants.

- For certain unusual spellings, it helps to say the word in your head as it should be phonetically pronounced. For instance, pronounce the 'c' in 'scissors' and the 'b' in 'climbed'.

- Divide longer words into syllables.

- Say the letters in a rhythm or to a tune.

- Draw a picture of the word to go with the spelling. Alternatively, write the letters in a distinctive shape or particular colours. If there are some unexpected letters in a word, they could be written in a different colour.

- Learn 'word families' together – e.g. 'knight, fight, bright, might'.

- Link words that have spellings in common in a story, such as: 'The **knight knew** that his **knees** were **knocking** as he undid the **knot** in his **knitting** with a flick of his **knife**.' It also helps to draw a picture of the story.

Phonic Skills

One of the difficulties commonly associated with dyslexia is poor phonological awareness – i.e. difficulties hearing the different sounds within words. Revising phonic skills is an effective strategy for most children who initially find literacy difficult. There is a wide range of resources available that go through the common phonic sounds and provide children with opportunities to decode phonologically regular words. I have found the following schemes helpful: **WordBlaze**, **The Nessy Learning Programme** and **Alpha to Omega**.

- Research by Solity and Vousden (2009) indicates that when children find literacy persistently difficult, it is most productive to teach them the most common way that letters are pronounced, rather than all the different options that occur in the English language. It is best to focus on the pronunciations that they will encounter most frequently, while also developing the pupil's vocabulary and knowledge of high-frequency words. Less common phonic spellings are often learnt as whole words, supported by the child's knowledge of vocabulary and the context of the sentence.

- Some children have difficulties correctly pronouncing words when speaking, which may make it more challenging for them to sound out words accurately when reading and writing. Adults can help by modelling correct pronunciation. For instance, if the child says, 'Big clee', the adult can repeat, 'Yes, a big tree', so that the child hears the correct pronunciation without being reprimanded for the error. Children who have significant difficulties with pronunciation could be referred to a speech and language therapist.

Informal activities to promote phonological awareness include:

• Identifying rhyming words, or words that start with the same sound.

• I spy with my little eye something beginning with . . .

• Clapping the syllables in words.

• Building words and nonsense words using letter tiles or flash cards.

• Synthesising and segmenting words – i.e. putting together individual sounds to make a word ('c-a-t' makes 'cat') and breaking words into individual sounds. For instance, what sounds can you hear in the word 'cat'?

• Practise listening to similar words and identifying which is correct. For instance, is it time for beg, or is it time for bed?

• Sound deletion: say 'bed' without the 'b'.

• Sound substitution: change the first sound of 'bed' to a 't'.

Working Memory

Working memory is the ability to retain information while we manipulate and use that information. For instance, it is necessary to be able to remember a sum while we work it out or to retain an instruction while we complete the task. Difficulties with working memory (particularly verbal memory) are often observed in learners who experience persistent literacy difficulties. Working memory problems can also interact with slow speed of processing because if it takes a little longer to process information, there is a greater risk of the information being forgotten. Therefore, there is considerable overlap between strategies that support working memory and those to support speed of processing.

Gathercole and Alloway (2009) suggest a range of strategies to support working memory. Some of these, along with other strategies that may be useful, are included below:

- Long instructions could be broken down into manageable chunks.

- Prompts could be given to remind the children about what needs to be completed. These may be recorded on to an audio device, written as bullet points or communicated through photos, pictures or symbols.

- It is helpful to monitor the memory load for each task. For instance, if the aim is to learn the procedure for multiplication, reduce the working memory load by providing the children with a multiplication table showing the answers to the times tables.

- Ensure that any equipment used to support learning is easily accessible at learners' desks so that their attention is not disrupted by having to fetch equipment.

- Ensure that there are strong class routines, so that routine information will be kept in long-term memory and not take up space in short-term memory.

- Ask children about *how* they remember best and then teach them memory strategies such as mnemonics, writing lists, mind maps, drawing diagrams or using picture prompts. This encourages meta-memory – awareness and understanding of one's own memory, which makes it easier to use memory effectively.

- Link new information to something that the pupils have already learnt so that they can fit the new information into the 'bigger picture'. This helps to transfer it to long-term memory.

- Provide regular opportunities for learning through 'doing' (such as a practical 'hands-on' activity) rather than learning by listening.

Speed of Processing

- There is currently little evidence to show that speed of verbal processing can be increased through training programmes. Therefore, it is important that adults make allowances for children who are slow to process verbal information. For instance, they may need additional thinking time when responding to mental maths items or difficult questions in class.

- Adults should monitor the speed of their speech and try to talk steadily when delivering important information, to give learners time to process what has been said.

- Providing important information in short chunks is helpful, perhaps giving only one or two instructions at a time so that learners are not overwhelmed by the amount of language that needs to be processed.

- Verbal information can be supported with visual prompts so that learners have a visual reminder of what has to be remembered. Visual prompts might include gestures, facial expressions and other forms of non-verbal communication; pictures, symbols, photographs, mind maps and diagrams; bullet points or key words (if the child can read); film clips, demonstrations and 'hands-on' activities.

- Adults should be aware that a slow speed of verbal processing often puts pressure on working memory skills because the information has to be retained for longer than is typical while the person processes it. Hence, it may be necessary to repeat information if the child has not retained what has been said.

- When starting a task, it may be helpful to ask the learner to explain what he/she has been asked to do. The process of explaining the activity will help to cement it in the learner's memory and will also highlight to the adult if there are parts of the task that have not been understood.

- Some learners are slow to process the symbols that they see. This may make it difficult for them to read fluently and also to process lots of visual information at once. For instance, reading piano music may be challenging, because perhaps six notes may need to be played at once compared with the trumpet where only one note is played at a time. Regular practice can help with speed of visual processing because the more the brain becomes accustomed to visually processing text, the more automatic the process is likely to become.

Executive Function

Executive function is a set of mental skills that include working memory, flexible thinking and self-control. We use these skills every day to learn, work and manage daily life. Problems with executive function can make it hard to plan, organise and sequence work. It may also make it hard for pupils to focus, follow directions and handle emotions, among other things.

Learners who find it difficult to mentally organise themselves to think, plan and effectively carry out tasks may show inconsistent performance. They may be able to read and talk well but find it difficult to put the individual skills together to write an essay or summarise some information. Likewise, a child may be able to do the individual skills of dressing, finding wet-weather gear and making a packed lunch, but may struggle to plan what is needed and do all the tasks together within a time limit prior to a day out.

Children who experience poor executive function skills may benefit from the following strategies:

- Breaking tasks down into stages and reducing the number of processes involved in difficult activities will help learners to structure and organise their ideas when completing complex tasks. This will make it less likely that the learner will feel overwhelmed and hence struggle to start the task.

- Providing essay structures, writing frames and sentence starters can help learners to complete written tasks.

- It may help to pre-teach some typical task sequences. For instance, a tick chart could be drawn up showing all the steps that the child needs to complete each morning before school. Helping children to see the order in which the activities need to be done, and having a visual reminder so that they can mentally tick off each item, should enable them to get ready more independently.

- A similar strategy can be employed in school using the child's timetable as a prompt. It would help if the timetable was annotated to include all the equipment that the child regularly needs each day in a typical week.

- A positive reward system could be put in place to motivate younger children to develop good organisational habits. For instance, they could earn tokens/praise for packing their bags and preparing other equipment each night, for completing parts of the morning routine within a given timescale, for recording and completing homework assignments effectively. In cases where learners have difficulty writing down what they need to do for homework, they should be supported in using other methods, such as audio-recording the teacher's directions, taking a screenshot of instructions or asking an adult to scribe.

- Children who have little concept of time may need to be explicitly taught about how the year is structured – for instance, the passing of the seasons, which months fit into which season, how this correlates to school terms, half-terms and weekends. The school timetable could be used to show the structure of a school day and week, highlighting meal and break times, the lengths of lessons, etc. When learners find telling the time challenging, it may help to start with teaching the time digitally before moving on to being able to read analogue clocks.

- Several books are available suggesting strategies to support executive function skills including:

  - *Executive Skills in Children and Adolescents: A Practical Guide to Assessment and Intervention* (3rd edition) by Peg Dawson and Richard Guare (Guilford Press, 2018)

  - *Smart but Scattered* by Peg Dawson and Richard Guare (Guilford Press, 2009)

  - *Executive Function in the Classroom: Practical Strategies for Improving Performance and Enhancing Skills for All Students* by Christopher Kaufman (Paul H. Brookes Publishing, 2010).

7. Conclusion

A Nasty Dose of the Yawns and other stories in the *Adventures with Diversity* series use humour, an adventurous spirit and the power of storytelling to aid understanding of the issues faced by children experiencing special educational needs.

This guide highlights the issues that may be faced by children with persistent difficulties with literacy/dyslexia. In addition to the practical problems of finding it hard to read and write in a literate society, it is clear that dyslexia can have negative social, emotional and mental health consequences. However, these can be greatly reduced by recognising the child's challenges and providing additional support. For many children, revision of phonic skills and some additional reading and writing practice may be all that is needed. For those children who continue to make limited progress despite appropriate intervention, longer-term support may be required. This is likely to be most effective when parents and teachers work together to provide consistent support.

It is encouraging that there is now a wide range of technology available to help people who find literacy difficult, including spelling and grammar checks when typing, speech-to-text software and audiobooks. The availability of assistive technology, alongside improved recognition of specific difficulties with literacy, should mean that the dyslexic children of today will be spared many of the emotional challenges that were faced by those who found the acquisition of literacy difficult in previous generations.

DOI: 10.4324/9781003208075-7

References

Bennett, K. (2008). 'Could do better': Improving literacy in schools. In Singleton, C. (Ed.) *The Dyslexia Handbook 2008/9.* The British Dyslexia Association.

British Dyslexia Association. (2010). About Dyslexia. www.bdadyslexia. org.uk/dyslexia/about-dyslexia/what-is-dyslexia (accessed 21 May 2021).

Crisfield, J. (1996). *The Dyslexia Handbook.* British Dyslexia Association.

Elliott, J.G. & Grigorenko, E.L. (2014). *The Dyslexia Debate.* Cambidge Univeristy Press.

Gathercole, S.E. & Alloway, T.P. (2009). *Working Memory and Learning: A Practical Guide for Teachers.* Sage.

Gross, J. (Ed.). (2008). *Getting in Early: Primary Schools and Early Intervention.* The Smith Institute and the Centre for Social Justice.

Humphrey, N. & Mullins, P.M. (2002). Personal constructs and attribution for academic success and failure in dyslexia. *British Journal of Special Education,* 29(4): 196–203.

Lima, R. (2011). Depressive symptoms and cognitive functions in children with developmental dyslexia. *Arquivos De Neuro-Psiquiatria,* 69(5): 845–854.

Livingston, E. M., Siegel, L. S. & Ribary, U. (2018). Developmental dyslexia: Emotional impact and consequences. *Australian Journal of Learning Difficulties,* 23(2): 107–135.

Macrotrends. (2020). UK Literacy rate – 2020. www.macrotrends.net/ countries/GBR/united-kingdom/literacy-rate (accessed 23 October 2020).

McNulty, M.A. (2003). Dyslexia and the life course. *Journal of Learning Disabilities*, 36(4): 363–381.

Milne, D. (2005). *Teaching the Brain to Read*. SK Publishing.

Moran, T.P. (2016). Anxiety and working memory capacity: A meta-analysis and narrative review. *Psychological Bulletin*, 142(8): 831–864.

Pollack, D. (2008). Dyslexia and self-esteem. In Singleton, C. (Ed.) *The Dyslexia Handbook 2008/9*. The British Dyslexia Association.

Riddick, B. (2010). *Living with Dyslexia: The Social and Emotional Consequences of Specific Learning Difficulties*. 2nd Edition. Routledge.

Rose, J. (2009). *Identifying and Teaching Children and Young People with Dyslexia and Literacy Difficulties*. DCSF Publications.

Roser, M. & Ortiz-Ospina, E. (2018). Our World in Data, Historical Change in Literacy. https://ourworldindata.org/literacy#historical-change-in-literacy (accessed 21 October 2020).

Snowling, M.J., Gooch, D.C., Hulme, C. & Nash, H.M. (2019). Developmental outcomes for children at high risk of dyslexia and children with developmental language disorder. *Child Development*, 90(5): 548–564.

Snyder, H. (2013). Major depressive disorders associated with broad impairments on neuropsychological measures of executive function: A meta-analysis and review. *Psychological Bulletin*, 139(1): 81–132.

Solity, J. & Vousden, J. (2009). Real books vs reading schemes: A new perspective from instructional psychology. *Educational Psychology*, 29(4): 469–511.

Topping, K. (1987). Paired reading: A powerful technique for parent use. *The Reading Teacher*, 40(7) 608–614.